Book 2

Beyond the Romantic Spirit

1880–1922

Selected, edited and annotated by Nancy Bachus

16 Intermediate to Early Advanced Piano Solos Reflecting the Influence of 16 Great Composers on Music at the Turn of the 20th Century

Alfred

ISBN 0-7390-3326-3

Cover art: *Interior with Piano*
by Fernand Lantoine (1876–1936)
Waterhouse and Dodd, London, Great Britain
Fine Art Photographic Library, London/Art Resource, New York

Contents

The author wishes to thank Mr. David Coppen at the Sibley Music Library for his cooperation, and Sharon Aaronson and E. L. Lancaster for their expertise and guidance throughout this entire series.

Foreword

To understand and interpret musical style, one must recapture the spirit of the environment in which composers lived, created and performed, and be aware of influential events of the time. As composers approached the 20th century, the piano had a 200-year history, and its popularity had grown with the rise of the middle class. The feats of virtuoso performers added to its mystique and contributed to the desire of musical amateurs to learn to play. Its range was both higher and lower than any orchestral instrument, and pianos could recreate orchestral music as well as simple songs. At the peak of its popularity, from 1880 to the early 1920s, the piano was at the center of entertainment in most middle- and upper-class homes as phonographs and radios were not yet common. The piano had great musical versatility including the capacity to touch the human spirit.

"The pianoforte is the most important of all musical instruments. Its invention was to music what the invention of printing was to poetry."
George Bernard Shaw (1856–1950), writer and music critic[1]

As the printing press brought literature to the world, the piano helped bring music out of the exclusive domain of the aristocracy and disseminated all types of music to the general public.

- The first pianos, developed by **Bartolomeo Cristofori** (1655–1731) around 1700, weighed less than the iron plate of a late 19th-century instrument. This piano was a development of the Industrial Revolution with thousands of manufactured and handmade parts.
- More than 350 different piano makers in the United States alone manufactured 400,000 instruments in 1909. Mass merchandising made them easy to purchase in stores, through mail-order catalogs, and even from door-to-door salesmen.
- At the turn of the 20th century, piano music was available for virtuosos as well as for teaching, playing for pleasure, singing, and dancing.
- *Beyond the Romantic Spirit*, Book 2, presents piano pieces from this period in a wide range of styles with music originating in Russia, England, France, Finland, Hungary, and North and South America.

Warshaw Collection
Pianos, Archives Center, NMAH
Smithsonian Institution

Traveling salesmen sometimes left a piano at a rural home for a few days while their car (specially designed to carry a piano) was being repaired! A piano sale was frequently negotiated upon the return.

[1] James R. Gaines, ed., *The Lives of the Piano* (New York: Holt, Rinehart and Winston, 1981), 41.

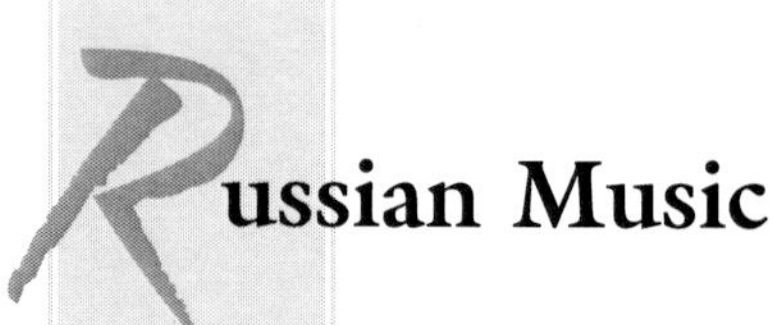

Russian Music

Until the 19th century, musicians imported from France, Germany and Italy created most art music in Russia, and native Russians traveled to Europe for serious music study. *A Life for the Czar* (1836), an opera by **Mikhail Glinka** (1804–1857), stimulated nationalist interest. In 1862, the first professional music school, the **St Petersburg Conservatory**, was founded by **Anton Rubinstein** (1829–1894) to *"create Russian musicians, instrumentalists and composers."*[3] Four years later, his brother **Nikolay Rubinstein** (1835–1881) founded the **Moscow Conservatory**.

Moscow Conservatory of Music

Vladimir Rebikov (1866–1920)

Vladimir Rebikov was known as a pianist in Russia and abroad. He composed operas, ballets, orchestral suites, and several musico-psychological dramas, but his many outstanding piano miniatures are what have remained in the repertoire.

- Born in Siberia, Rebikov studied at the Moscow Conservatory and in Berlin and Vienna. He eventually settled in Moscow but traveled abroad for concert tours.
- His early works show the influence of **Peter Tchaikovsky** (1840–1893). (Tchaikovsky graduated from St. Petersburg and then taught at the Moscow Conservatory.) Around 1900, Rebikov began experimenting with more modern harmonies such as **bitonality** (two keys simultaneously), **whole-tone scales** and other techniques.
- Rebikov believed *"music is the language of the emotions"*[4] and that its purpose is to transmit this to a listener through sounds. Furthermore, forms and traditions should not restrict music since feelings are not limited, and music begins where words are inadequate.

[2] M. Montagu-Nathan, *Contemporary Russian Composers* (London: Cecil Palmer & Hayward, 1917), 181.

[3] Elsa Z. Posell, *Russian Composers* (Boston: Houghton Mifflin Company, 1967), 8.

[4] Montagu-Nathan, *Contemporary Russian Composers,* 184.

Danse caractéristique

Vladimir Rebikov (1866–1920)
Op. 2, No. 6

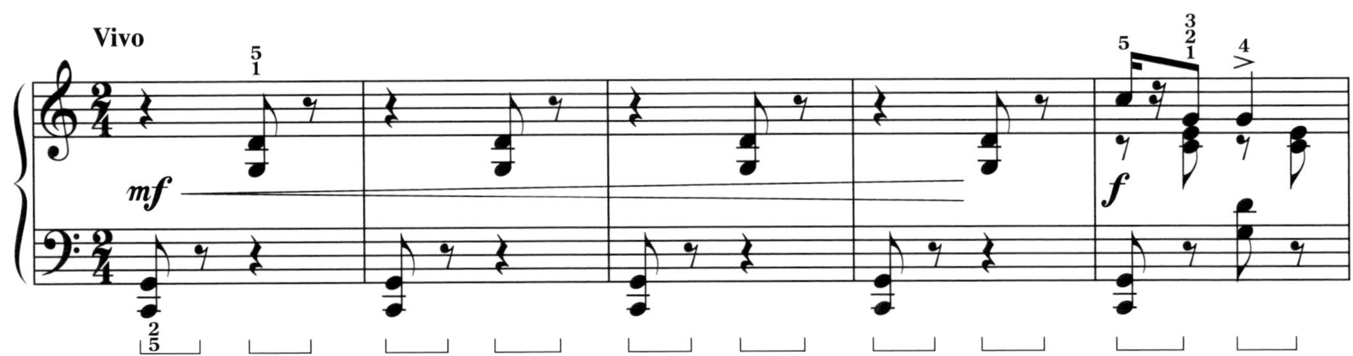

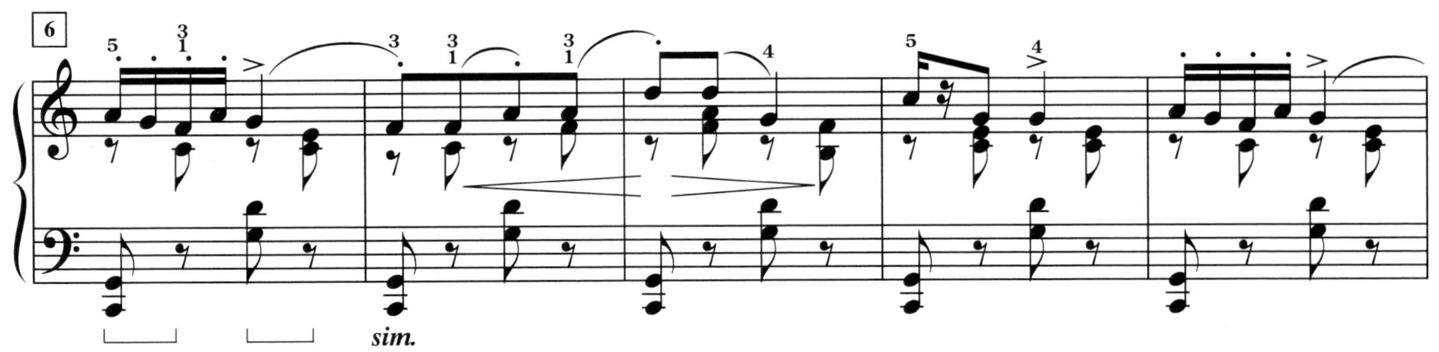

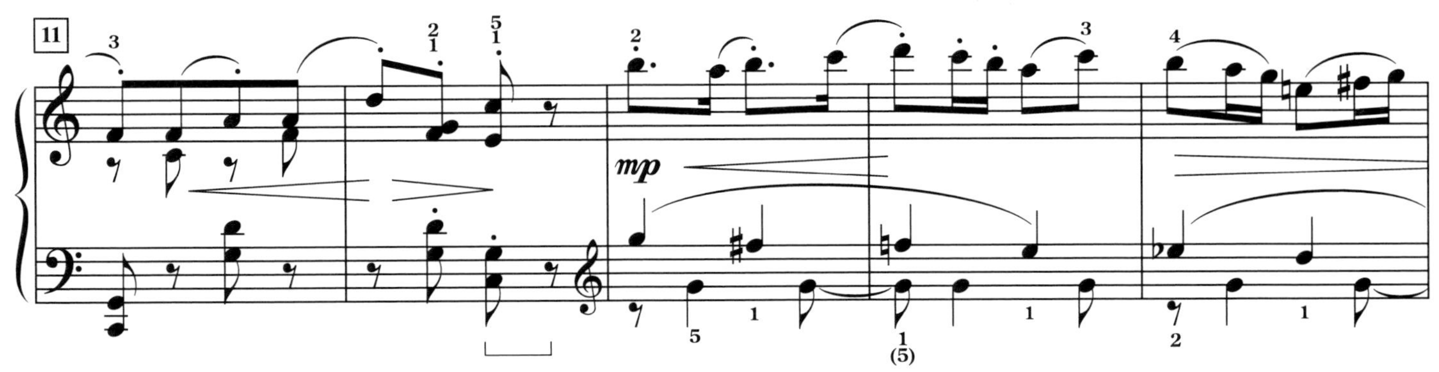

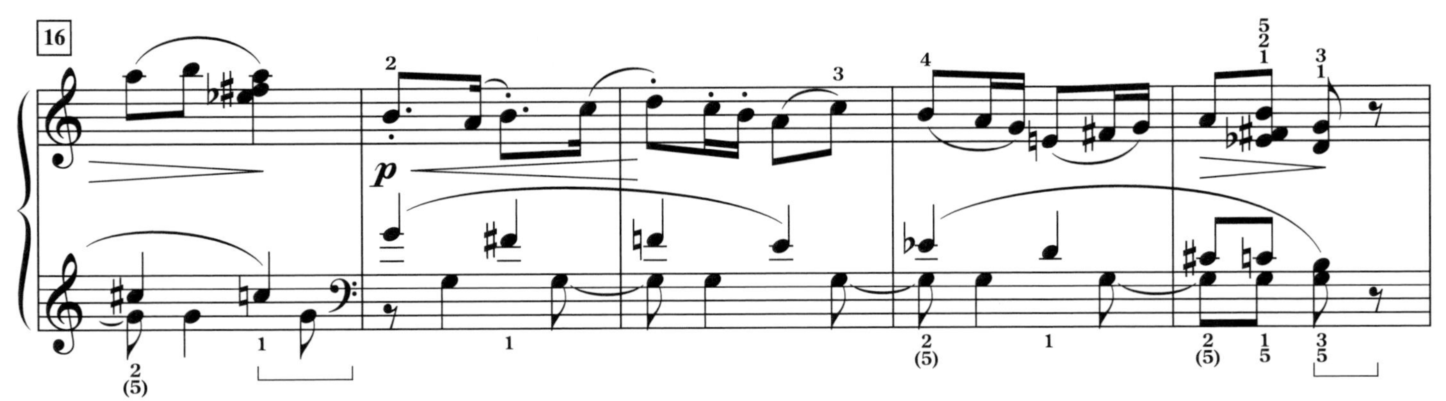

Meno mosso
LH above RH
sim.
Tempo I

51
mp
56
p
61
f
sim.
f
8va
66
cresc. e accel.
72
ff
mf
p

"I was once a Chopinist, then a Wagnerist, now I am only a Scriabinist."
Alexander Scriabin[5]

Alexander Scriabin (1872–1915)

In **Alexander Scriabin's** brief lifetime, he was known mainly for his orchestral works. Today his 10 piano sonatas and about 200 shorter pieces are recognized for their soulful melodies, originality and musical value. He developed his own harmonic system and has been called *"a visionary who lost touch with reality."*[6]

- Scriabin and his distant cousin **Sergei Rachmaninoff** (1873–1943) both attended the Moscow Conservatory where Scriabin was hailed as "Russia's Chopin." Beginning in a late Romantic style, his last works approach atonality.
- His egomania was evident when he refused "corrections" to one of his works, forcing his composition teacher **Anton Arensky** (1861–1906) to fail him. He won the Little Gold Medal in piano but never received a diploma in composition.
- Scriabin saw the artist (himself) as a redeemer and prophet whose purpose was to create music to give *"a glimpse of higher spiritual planes."*[7] He wrote, *"I am God, I am the world, I am the center of the universe."*[8] His philosophies were united with music in *The Poem of Ecstasy* (1908) and *Prometheus, The Poem of Fire* (1910), the world's first multi-media composition. The score used a "color organ" that would flash colors into the hall synchronized with the music.
- He worked 12 years on *Mystery*, a synthesis of the arts, to be performed in a specially built amphitheater in India at the foot of the Himalayas. Scored for orchestra and a 2,000-voice chorus, it included dancers, poetry, color keyboard, perfumes, incense, and bells suspended from zeppelins (blimps). Intended to bring about the regeneration of the world and the purification of mankind, it was never completed.
- The Russian-born virtuoso pianist **Vladimir Horowitz** (1903–1989) at age 11 played for Scriabin and also heard him perform. Horowitz frequently used Scriabin's *Vers la Flamme* (Toward the Flame), Op. 72, as an encore.

[5] Derek Watson, ed., intro. and selection, *Dictionary of Musical Quotations* (Ware Hertfordshire: Cumberland House, Wordsworth Editions Ltd., 1994), 188.

[6] Posell, *Russian Composers,* 74.

[7] Joseph Machlis, *Introduction to Contemporary Music* (New York: W. W. Norton & Co., Inc., 1961), 100.

[8] John Gillespie, *Five Centuries of Keyboard Music* (Belmont, CA: Wadsworth Publishing, 1965), 272.

Prelude in G Major

Alexander Scriabin (1872–1915)
Op. 13, No. 3

ⓐ The RH chord on beat 1 of measures 8, 12, 16 and 18 may be rolled, if necessary, to play all the notes.

"I cannot cast out the old way of writing and … acquire the new. I have made intense efforts to feel the musical manner of today, but it will not come to me."

Sergei Rachmaninoff[9]

Sergei Rachmaninoff (1873–1943)

Sergei Rachmaninoff was known as a composer, conductor and piano virtuoso. He wrote operas, symphonies, chamber music, choral works, songs and many works for piano. Because his compositional style reflects 19th-century Romanticism, many scholars dismiss his works, but his piano preludes and concertos never lost popularity with the public.

- Due to his great talent and lack of diligence, at age 12 Rachmaninoff was sent to Moscow to live in the home of the piano teacher **Nikolay Zverev,** who structured a 16-hour day for the gifted students he accepted. (Scriabin was a fellow student.) **Peter Tchaikovsky** visited frequently and became Rachmaninoff's idol.
- At the Moscow Conservatory his piano professor, **Alexander Ziloti** (1863–1945), had studied with **Franz Liszt** (1811–1886). As a student, Rachmaninoff memorized and performed difficult piano compositions within a few days, was a brilliant sight-reader, and was able to transpose easily. At his graduation, he was awarded the Great Gold Medal (for excellence in both piano and composition), the conservatory's highest honor.
- The *Prelude in C-sharp Minor,* Op. 3, No. 2 ("Moscow Bells"), brought him international fame when it was published in 1892. However, there was no accompanying fortune because he sold it for a flat fee without royalties.
- In 1915 when Scriabin suddenly died (of blood poisoning from a boil), Rachmaninoff played recitals of Scriabin's music to raise money for his family. This launched Rachmaninoff's career as a concert pianist, since before this he had performed only his own music in public. He became known as one of the great pianists of the 20th century.
- After the Bolshevik Revolution in 1917, he left Russia and settled in the United States. Refusing major conducting positions, he earned his living as a pianist. His remote, even gloomy appearance hid the warm, sensitive nature evident in his playing. A meticulous perfectionist, he was never satisfied with his artistic achievements.

[9] Ian Crofton & Donald Fraser, *A Dictionary of Musical Quotations* (New York: Schirmer Books, 1985), 122.

Rachmaninoff wrote two sets of pieces (Op. 33 and Op. 39) entitled *Etudes-tableaux* (Studies-Pictures), a term he originated. These pieces tend to grow from a single musical idea and are more chromatic than his *Preludes.* Through technical brilliance, each work depicts a scene or picture, but the details were never revealed. Rachmaninoff said, *"I do not believe in the artist disclosing too much of his images. Let them [listeners] paint for themselves what it most suggests."*[10]

Etude-tableau in G Minor

Sergei Rachmaninoff (1873–1943)

Op. 33, No. 8

[10] David Dubal, *The Art of the Piano* (New York: Summit Books, Simon & Schuster, Inc., 1989), 385.

10
p
mf
p
mf
12
dim.
p
mf
14
p
mf
cresc.
16
f
pp
19
mf
dim.

22
pp
poco rit.
24
cresc.
veloce
f
26
ff
LH 4
27
28

29
rit.
30
ff
mf
32
8va
pp
f
p
pp
36
Tempo I
pp
mf
p
mf

38
dim.
p
mf
40
p
mf
p
cresc.
poco accel.
42
43
ff
sff
pp
half pedal

"I ... follow my own way ... and never do anything merely because of the accepted rules."
Sergei Prokofiev[11]

Sergei Prokofiev (1891–1953)

As a young man, **Sergei Prokofiev** was called *enfant terrible* and the "young barbarian" while today his music is some of the most recorded and performed of 20th-century composers. A brilliant pianist, his five concertos, nine sonatas, two sonatinas, and more than 100 short pieces have made a major contribution to the modern piano literature.

- Prokofiev's father managed a 15,000-acre estate in the Ukraine. His parents structured his activities and education with music a part of his daily life. At age nine he heard an opera in Moscow, wrote one the next year and staged and performed it with relatives. For two summers, Russian composer **Reinhold Glière** (1875–1956) lived at the estate and tutored him.
- At his entrance to the St. Petersburg Conservatory at age 13, Prokofiev presented four completed operas, two sonatas, a symphony and more than 60 piano pieces. Ten years younger than most students, he was rude, arrogant and argumentative. Early performances of his percussive *Suggestion Diabolique,* Op. 4, No. 4, and first Piano Concerto (1911) made him famous. Reviews stated he needed a strait jacket, and, *"This music is enough to drive you mad."* Others wrote, *"This is a genius ... what originality."*[12]
- After the Bolshevik Revolution in 1917, Prokofiev settled in Paris, but he moved back to Russia in 1936 with his wife and two sons. Encouraged by the Soviet government to return, Party leaders then publicly denounced all he had written in the West, as well as many of his new works, for having "Western formalist decay."
- In the late 1930s, about seven million Russians were sent to forced labor camps and a half million were executed[13] including a producer of one of Prokofiev's operas. His marriage was nullified in 1948, along with all those between Russian citizens and foreign-born nationals. That year his Spanish-born wife, **Lina Prokofiev** (1897–1989), was arrested for "espionage" and imprisoned for nine years. He never saw her again.
- Despite personal tragedies, many of his most beloved works were written after his return to Russia, including the *Romeo and Juliet* ballet and *Peter and the Wolf.*

Prokofiev described his composition style as having several elements: the **classical**, from hearing his mother practice Beethoven Sonatas; **innovation**, the harmonic language he developed to express strong emotions; the **toccata** or motor aspect, giving rhythmic vitality; **lyrical expression**, and the aspect of **"scherzo-ness"** or jest, laughter and mockery.

[11] Victor Seroff, *Sergei Prokofiev, A Soviet Tragedy* (New York: Taplinger Publishing Co., 1979), 74.

[12] Ibid., 65–66.

[13] <http://www.siue.edu/~aho/musov/proko/prokofiev3.html>

The 20 pieces of the *Visions Fugitives* were composed in 1917 and were inspired by a Russian poem, *"In every fugitive vision I see worlds, Full of the changing play of rainbow hues."*

Visions Fugitives No. 1

Sergei Prokofiev (1891–1953)
Op. 22, No. 1

"To be immediately understood means one is not worth understanding."
Cyril Scott[14]

English Music

After the death of **Henry Purcell** (1659–1695), there were no native English composers of significance for 200 years. Research by the ethnomusicologist **Cecil Sharp** (1859–1924) into native English folk songs and dances stimulated interest in national music, and a group of composers appeared in England at the turn of the 20th century including **Sir Edward Elgar** (1857–1934), **Frederick Delius** (1862–1934), **Ralph Vaughan Williams** (1872–1958), **Gustav Holst** (1874–1934), **Benjamin Britten** (1913–1976) and **Cyril Scott**.

Cyril Scott (1879–1970)

Cyril Scott was a composer, virtuoso pianist, conductor, poet, an author of seven books, and a nutritionist. He wrote operas, choral, chamber and orchestral works along with numerous songs and piano pieces. Although widely performed in the first half of the 20th century, many considered his music too modern. By the end of the century, it was thought not to be progressive enough and was seldom heard.

- Born in Cheshire, England, Scott was able to play any tune he heard and improvise before the age of three. At age 12, he was sent to Frankfurt, Germany to study for the first time and later spent three years there. He made his London debut in 1901 and soon signed contracts with two music publishers.

- In his early twenties, he became interested in Indian philosophy, theosophy, astrology, and the therapeutic value of herbs and natural foods. He wrote on all these and many other subjects, and also had several volumes of poetry published. Under the influence of Eastern mysticism, he wrote his popular piano piece *Lotus Land*. He toured throughout the world interpreting his own works.
- Believing in reincarnation, Scott felt he had lived previous lives. He had close associations with mediums, and claimed he communicated with spirits of the deceased in séances. He saw music as a means for mankind to reach a higher spiritual level.

[14] A. Eaglefield Hull, *Cyril Scott* (London: Kegan Paul, Trench, Trubner & Co., Ltd., 1918), 176.

The **waltz** was the most popular ballroom dance of the 19th century, and most major composers of the 19th and early 20th centuries used it in some way. Waltzes appeared as part of operas, operettas, ballets, and symphonic works, and also stood alone.

This waltz is the first of a set of three written in 1906. Scott's piano concerto, operas, and symphonies were overshadowed by the popularity of his songs and short piano pieces.

Little Waltz

Cyril Scott
(1879–1970)

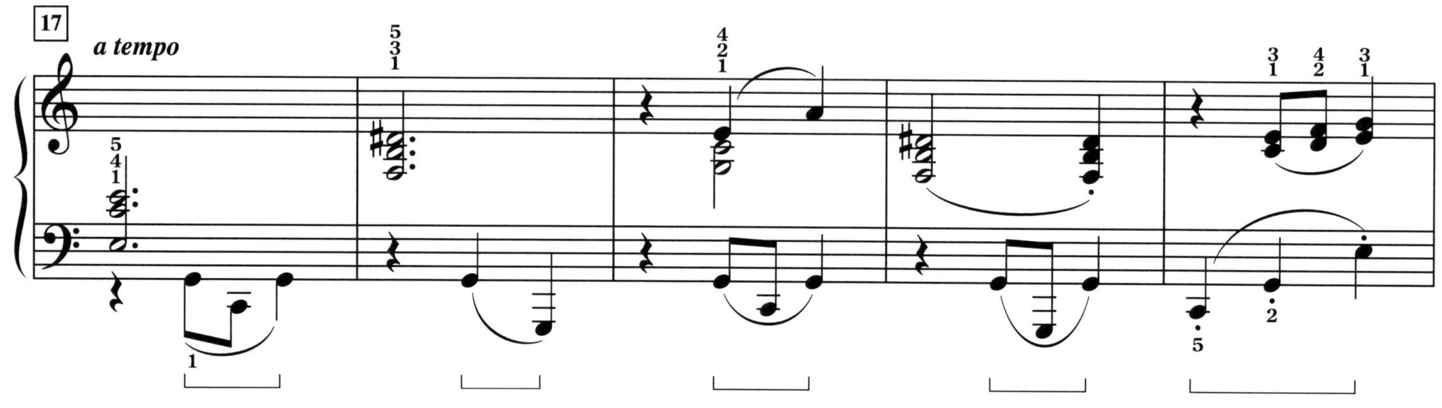

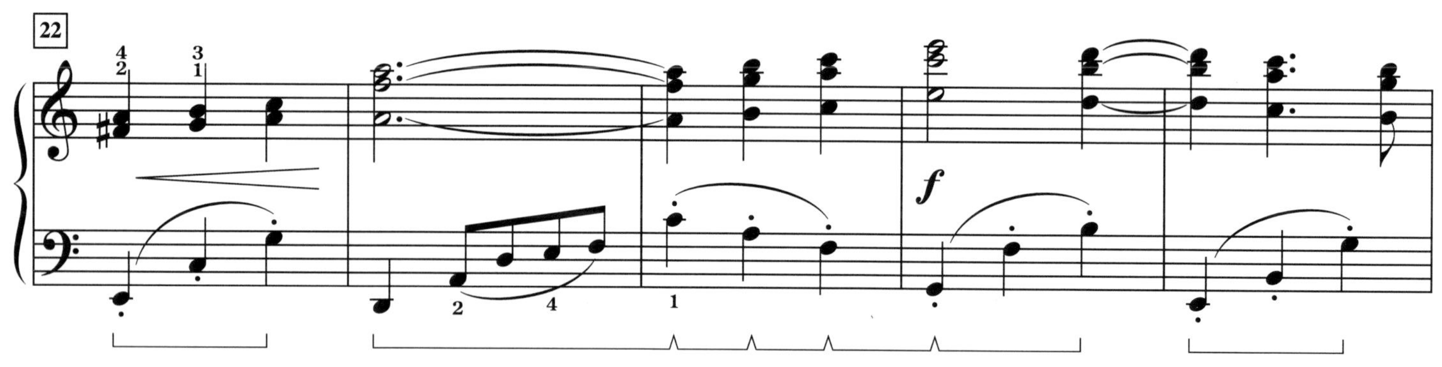

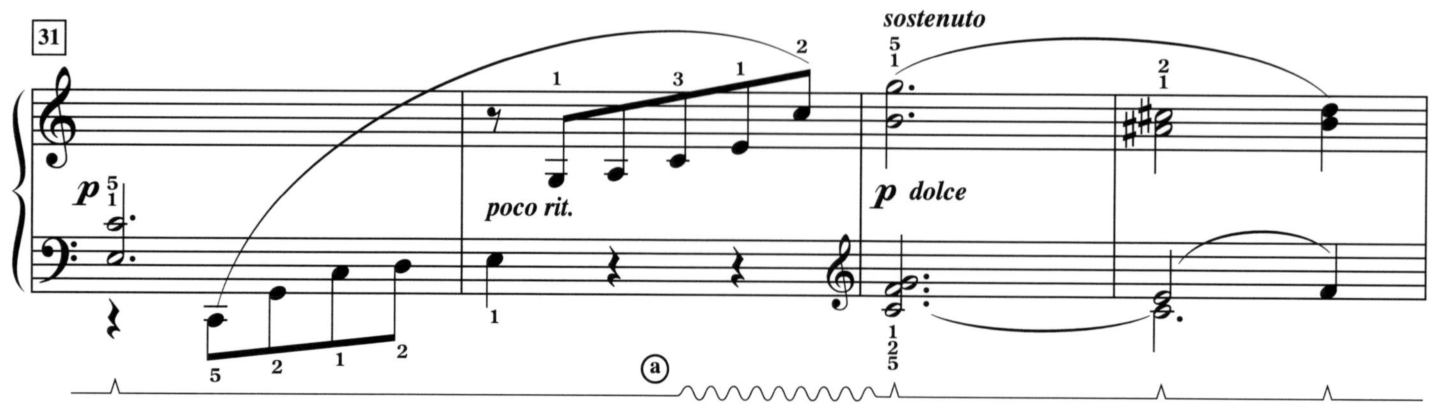

(a) Flutter the pedal to thin the texture.

35
40
45
f
50
D.C. al Coda
rit.
Coda
mf

"What makes their art French is a sense of the beauty of life and a desire to enjoy it with the senses. ...[They] approach life and music with joy and lightness."

Ilana Vered (b. 1943), concert pianist[15]

French Music

By the early 20th century, **Paris** was the **cultural capital of Europe**. **Claude Debussy's** (1862–1918) *Prélude à l'après-midi d'un faune* (Prelude to the Afternoon of a Faun) (1894) has been called the "first piece of 20th century music," and was influenced by French art and poetry. In Paris, the **Universal Exhibition of 1889** unveiled the Eiffel Tower to the world along with music and art of Eastern Europe and the South Pacific. In the early 1900s, Russian impresario **Sergei Diaghilev** (1872–1929) introduced Russian art exhibitions, concerts and ballets. Paris had become the center for musical innovation.

Gabriel Grovlez (1879–1944)

Gabriel Grovlez was active in Parisian musical life in the early 20th century as a pianist, composer and opera conductor. The charm of his instructional piano pieces has kept them in publication to the present day.

- Grovlez's first piano teacher was his mother who was the daughter of one of **Frédéric François Chopin's** (1810–1849) students. At the Paris Conservatory, Grovlez won a first prize in piano and studied composition with **Gabriel Fauré** (1845–1924). At the age of 20, he became a piano professor at the Schola Cantorum, a music school in Paris founded in 1884.
- In 1906 Grovlez presented the Parisian premiere of Maurice Ravel's (1875–1937) *Sonatine* for piano and also conducted the first performance of Ravel's *Ma mère l'oye* (Mother Goose) ballet.
- As a conductor in the leading theaters in Paris, he did many operatic revivals by early French composers such as **Jean-Baptiste Lully** (1632–1687) and **Jean-Philippe Rameau** (1683–1764). Grovlez was named Director of the Paris Opéra, and during his 20-year tenure, he also conducted operas in Cairo, Lisbon, New York, and Chicago.

Entrance to the Universal Exhibition of 1889 *by Jean Beraud (1849–1936)*

[15] Elaine Strauss, "The Colorful Palette of French Piano Music," *Clavier Magazine* (October 1995): 15.

A French poem precedes each of the eight pieces in *L'almanach aux images* (The Almanac of Pictures) by Grovlez with poem and piece sharing a title. The fourth composition, *Chanson du chasseur* (Song of the Hunter), celebrates the joys of hunting as experienced by both peasants and kings. It doesn't really matter if they return successful or empty-handed. The final line of the poem translates, *"Open your [hunting] bag!"* The call of "hunting horns" is heard in the opening and throughout the piece.

Chanson du chasseur

Gabriel Grovlez (1879–1944)
L'almanach aux images, No. 4

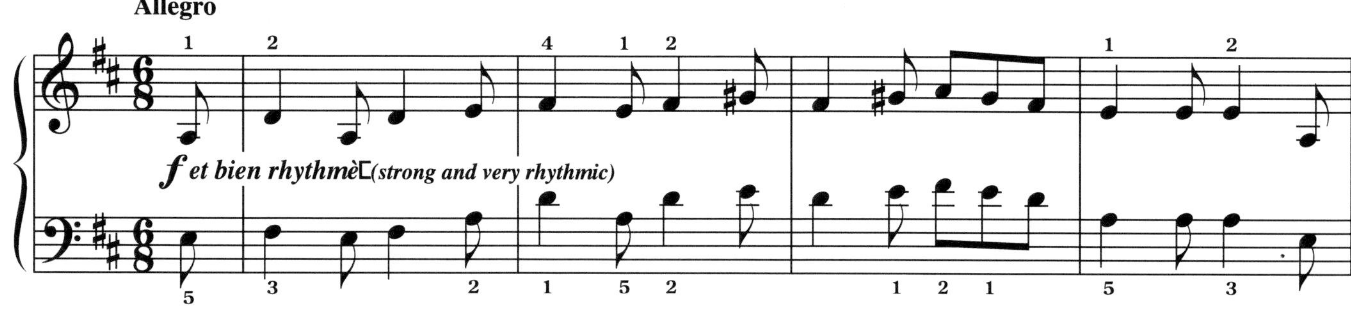

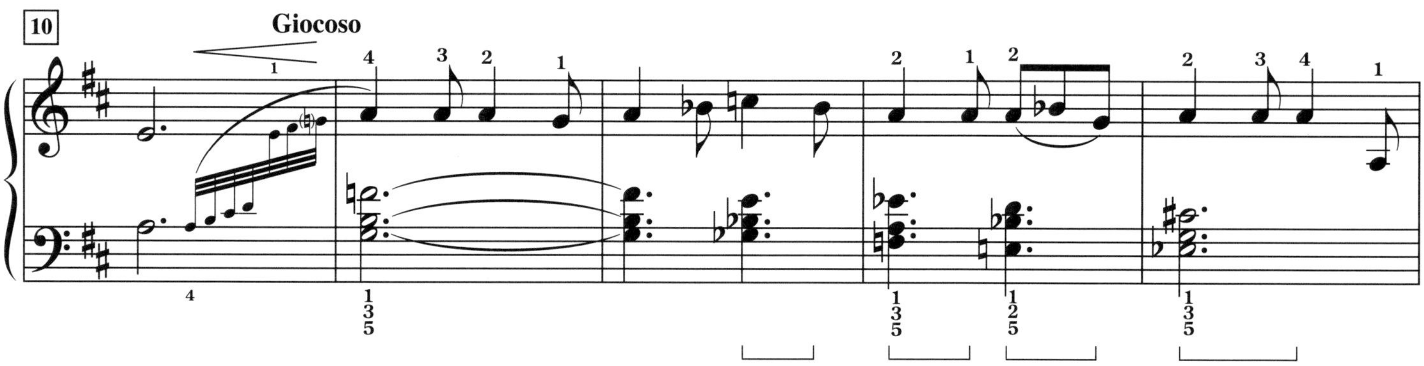

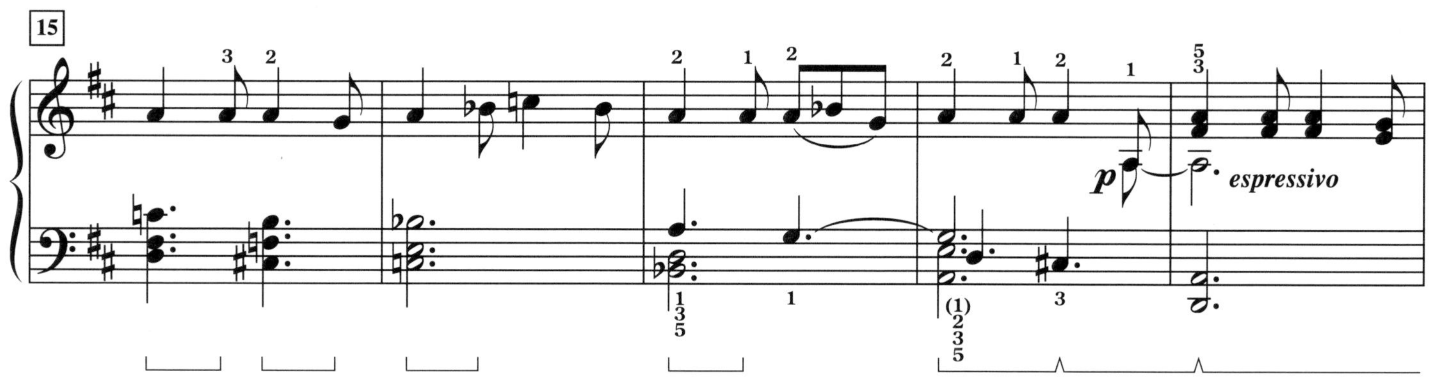

ⓐ The editor suggests all grace notes be played before the beat.

20
cédez légèrement (slower and lightly)
a tempo
u.c
t.c.
25
non legato
30
mf
35
cédez
a tempo
p
mf
u.c
t.c.
40
p espressivo

44
cresc.
49
p subito
u.c
cresc.
t.c.
55
f
cresc.
60
(les 8ves ad lib.) [the octaves are optional]
ff
65

70
espressivo
cédez
p subito
u.c
75
a tempo
cédez
t.c.
80
a tempo
p
dim.
u.c
85
ppp
90
RH over
Un peu retenu
(A little held back)
a tempo
en dehors, mais pp
(bring out, but softly)
ff
t.c.
les deux Pédales
(both pedals: u.c. and damper)

"I think and feel in sounds."
Maurice Ravel[16]

Maurice Ravel (1875–1937)

Maurice Ravel, the leading French composer after World War I, is considered to be one of the greatest piano composers of the 20th century. His orchestral works won him international fame with their brilliance and colorful scoring, and his piano pieces are part of any virtuoso's repertoire. He wrote relatively few compositions, but almost all are in the performing repertoire.

- Born in the Basque region of France near the Spanish border, Ravel was raised in Paris. His mother sang Spanish folk songs to him, nurturing a fascination for Spanish music, rhythms and folklore. These influences are present in many of his works.
- Although he was a student at the Paris Conservatory, Ravel never won the top compositional *Prix de Rome.*[17] When he was rejected the fourth time, his reputation as a composer was already so great that outraged musicians brought about the resignation of the conservatory director, making Ravel even more famous.
- He tried to enlist in the armed forces during World War I, but was rejected because he was underweight. (Only about five feet tall, Cyril Scott stated, *"He [Ravel] was so small and slender that if he had not been a composer he might have made an excellent jockey."*[18]) Still wanting to serve his country, he volunteered as an ambulance driver at the front lines taking wounded soldiers to medical care. Each movement of his *Le Tombeau de Couperin* for piano is dedicated to a friend who died in the war.
- Meticulously groomed, Ravel was always dressed elegantly, in the height of fashion with style and superb taste. His music has been described in much the same way—ultra-polished, suave, imaginative, and flawless in craftsmanship and proportion, with emotion perfectly controlled by the intellect.

Maurice Ravel (right) and Vaclav Nijinsky (1890–1950), the principal dancer and then choreographer for the Ballet Russe in Paris

[16] Nat Shapiro, ed., *An Encyclopedia of Quotations about Music* (New York: Da Capo Press, 1978), 56.

[17] This prize was awarded annually in music between 1803 and 1968, except during the two world wars, to a French composer under the age of 30, and was administered by the Paris Conservatory. Winners received financial support and a two- to five-year residency in Rome.

[18] Cyril Scott, *Bone of Contention: An Autobiography* (New York: Arco Publishing Co., 1969), 129.

Ravel *"summed up the whole era of the waltz [with his]* Valses nobles and sentimentales *that look back ... to the waltzes of Schubert"*[19] (who composed sets titled *Valses nobles* and *Valses sentimentales*). Composed for solo piano in 1911, two years later Ravel orchestrated his *Valses* and then arranged them as a ballet entitled, *Adélaïde, ou le langage des fleurs.*

The piano solo version was premiered at a concert of new music in Paris. Each work was presented anonymously to prevent the response to the works being influenced by the composer's name. The audience voted for a probable composer after the performance. The adventurous harmonies and complex rhythms in the *Valses* caused many to laugh and boo during the performance, and few named Ravel as the author.

This waltz, the second in the set, is "sentimental," tinged with nostalgia, and has one of the few indications in Ravel's works for the use of *rubato*.

Valses nobles et sentimentales No. 2

Maurice Ravel
(1875–1937)

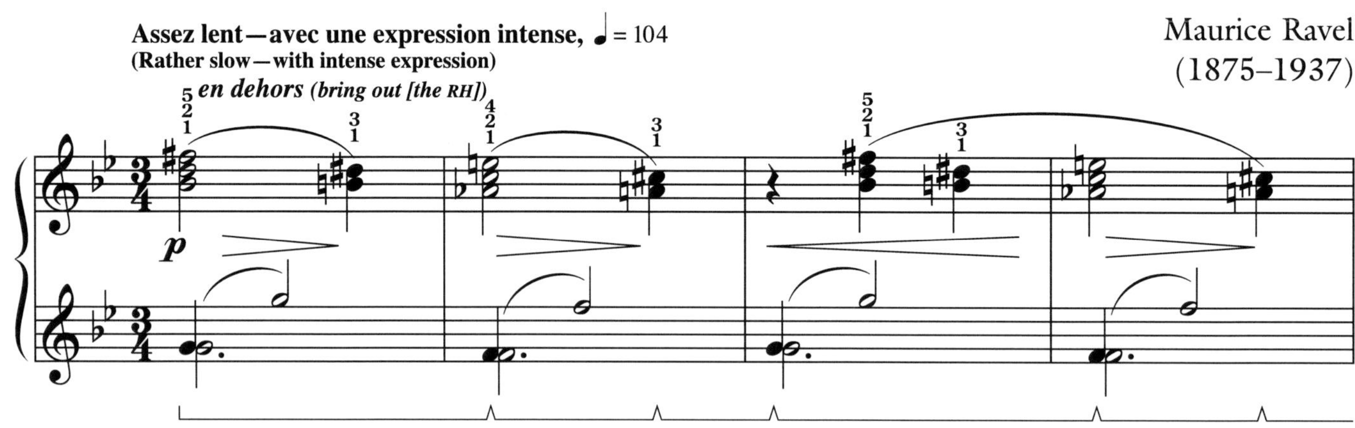

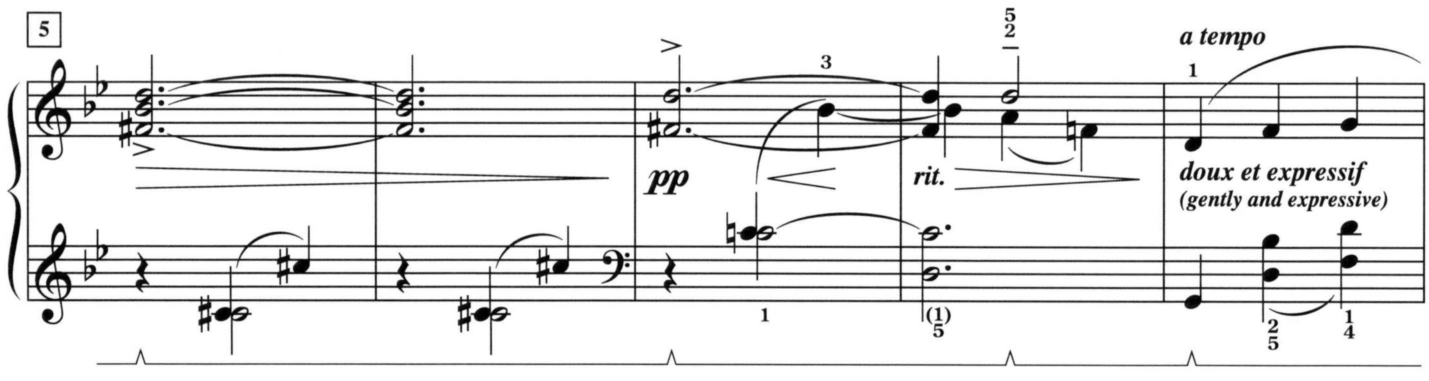

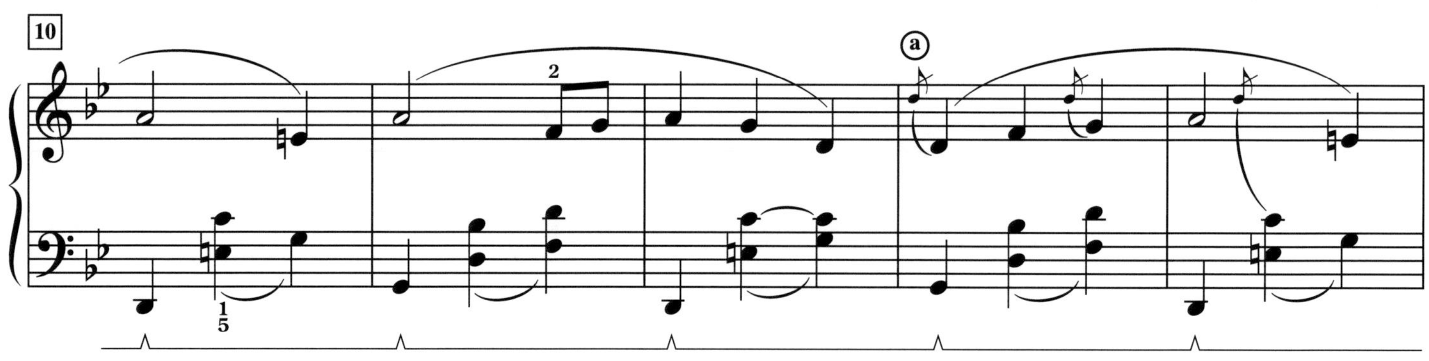

(a) The editor suggests all grace notes be played before the beat.

[19] *New Grove Dictionary of Music and Musicians,* s.v. "Waltz" (London: Macmillan, 1980).

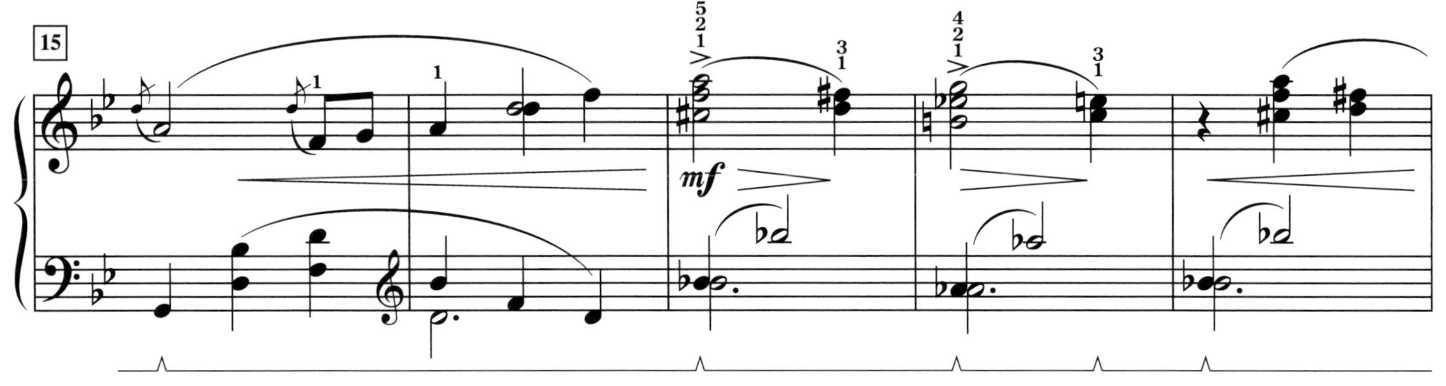

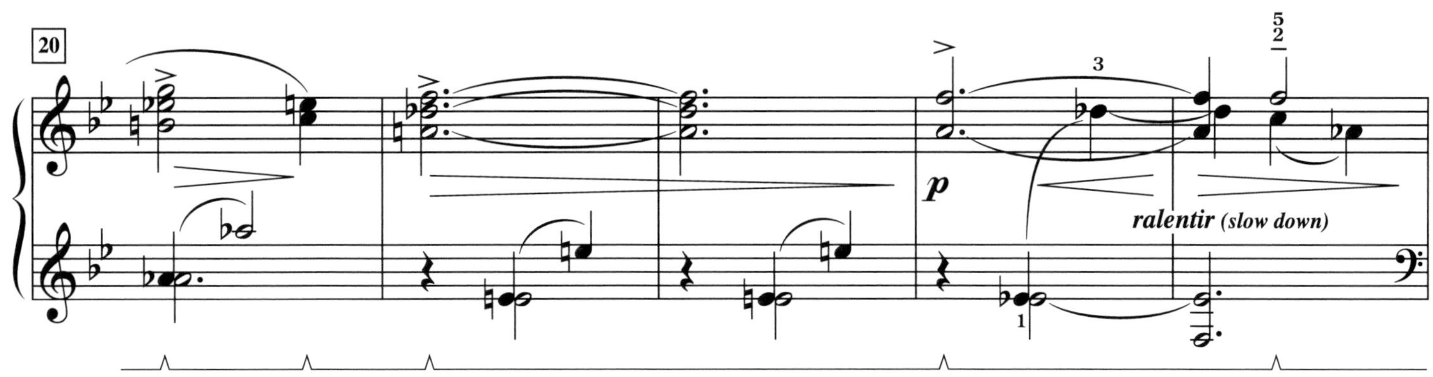

au mouvt (un peu plus lent et rubato)
(a tempo [a little slower and freely])

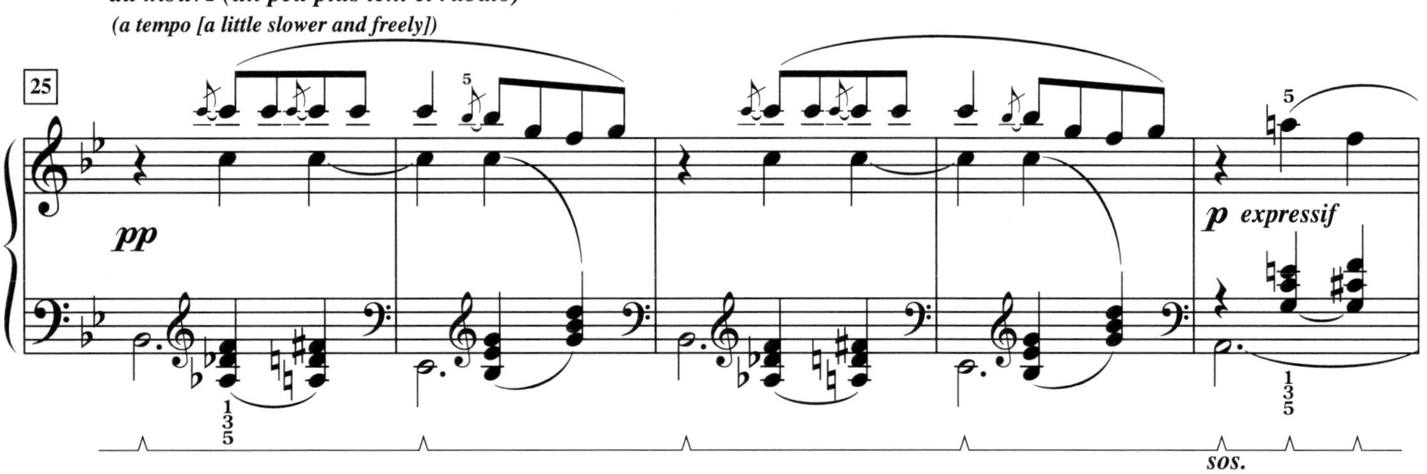

1er mouvt (Original tempo)

ⓑ The curved lines here and in measures 63 and 64 indicate that the sound should continue. Keeping the damper pedal depressed will allow the strings to vibrate and continue to ring.

36
41
mystérieux (mysterious)
pp un peu en dehors (bring out a little)
47
f très expressif
53
au mouvt
(rubato)
p
ralentir
pp
59
p expressif
ralentir
sos.
senza sos.

"You forgot that the piano had hammers when Debussy played ... and ... he achieved distinctive effects by the use of both pedals."
Léon Vallas (1879–1956), French critic [20]

Claude Debussy (1862–1918)

Many consider **Claude Debussy** to be the greatest French composer of all time and the most important composer for piano after **Franz Liszt** (1811–1886). His music exploits the tonal possibilities of the instrument in an original way. To express his impressions of the world in sound, Debussy *"create[s] pictures, images and illusions [that] can sometimes seem miraculous."*[21]

- Many of Debussy's composition professors at the Paris Conservatory were shocked at his unorthodox harmonies and disregard for textbook rules. More progressive teachers saw his genius, and as a result, he was awarded the *Prix de Rome* in 1884. During his residency in Rome, he met Franz Liszt and heard him play.
- The Universal Exhibition of 1889, and Debussy's associations with **Erik Satie** (1886–1925) and the Impressionist painters and Symbolist poets all impacted the development of his unique style. His *Prélude à l'après-midi d'un faune* for orchestra (1894) has been called the most original work in the history of music.
- *Rêverie* and *Clair de lune* are probably Debussy's best-known piano solos, but *Estampes* and *Images* show greater maturity. His 24 *Préludes* (two books of 12) are landmarks in the literature with their daring colors and atmospheric effects. They have been called scenes or "sense impressions" that *"seem to give the ear eyes."*[22] The evocative titles of his *Préludes*, like *Feux d'artifice* (Fireworks) and *Voiles* (Sails or Veils), are placed at the end.

Claude Debussy at the piano in the home of composer Ernest Chausson (1855–1899)

[20] Percy M. Young, *Keyboard Musicians of the World* (New York: Abelard-Schuman, 1968), 137.

[21] Paul Roberts, *Images, The Piano Music of Claude Debussy* (Portland, OR: Amadeus Press, 1996), 2.

[22] Ibid., 7.

Des pas sur la neige (Footsteps in the Snow) is the sixth prelude in the first book. Debussy's instructions at the beginning suggest that the repetitive left-hand motive, with its dissonance and resolution, could conjure an image of stumbling, snow-covered boots trudging wearily over a bleak, frozen landscape. The emotion of the sighing melody fluctuates and ends with cold loneliness. Writers frequently use images of ice and snow as a metaphor for spiritual desolation with its accompanying pain.

Des pas sur la neige

Claude Debussy (1862–1918)
Préludes, Book 1, No. 6

ⓐ Flutter the pedal to thin the texture.

13
Cédez (Slower)
pp
retenu (held back)
16
a tempo
pp
p
19
Cédez
più p
En animant surtout dans l'expression
(Becoming animated and with expression)
a tempo
pp
m.d.
p expressif et tendre
(expressing tenderness)
22
m.g.
(LH)
m.d.
sempre pp

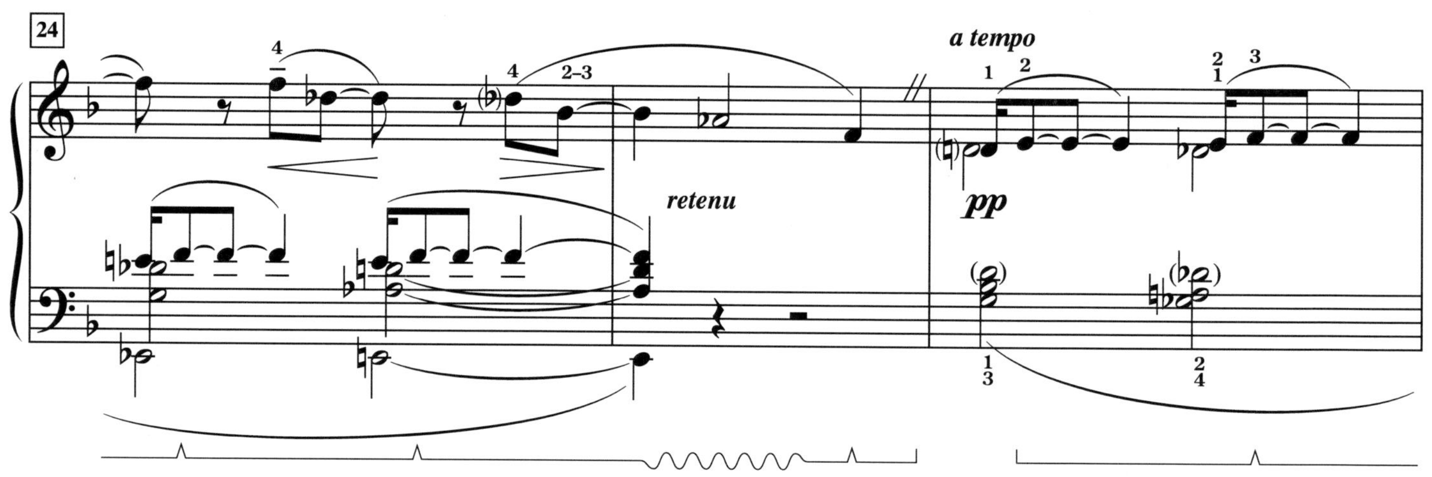

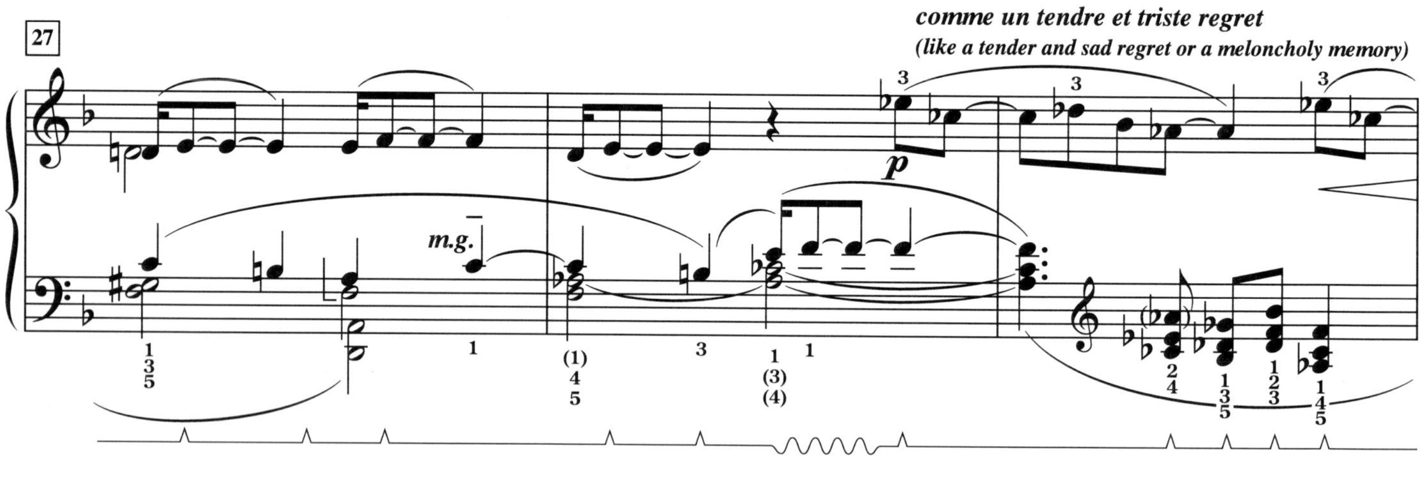

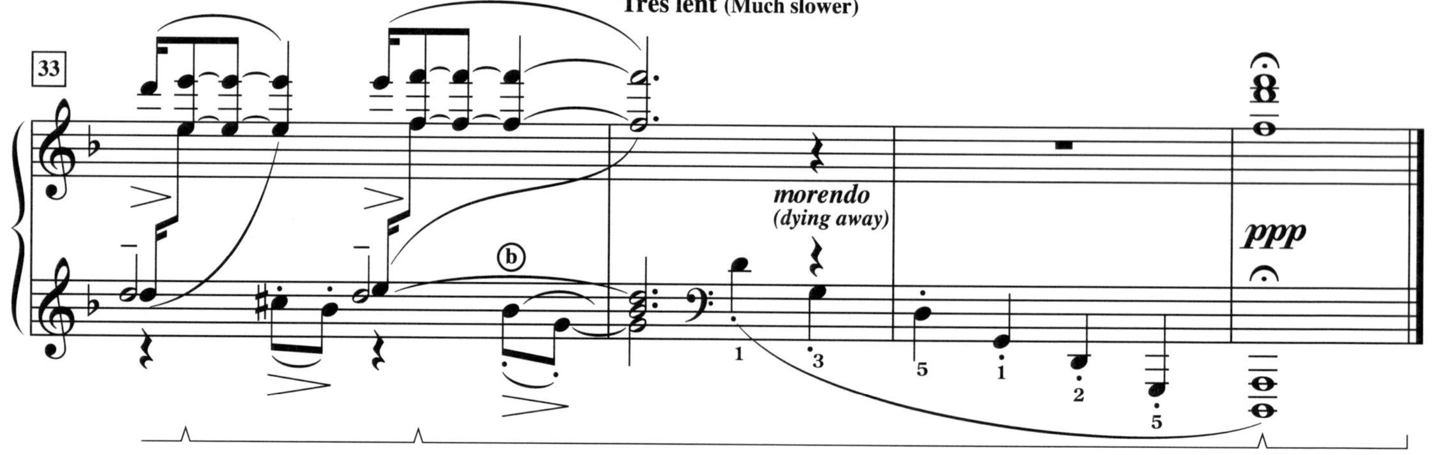

ⓑ The curved line on the B-flat indicates that the sound should continue. Keeping the damper pedal depressed will allow the strings to vibrate and continue to ring.

Jacques Ibert (1890–1962)

Jacques Ibert was a skilled arts administrator as well as a composer who wrote in Romantic, Impressionistic, and Neo-classic styles. Successful in almost all forms except oratorio, he wrote several operas, orchestral and choral music, a ballet, concertos, chamber music, songs, piano music, and scores for radio, films and music festivals. His music exhibits the French characteristics of clarity, elegance and wit.

- Born in Paris, Ibert took classes in drama and theater before deciding on a career in music. He studied composition at the Paris Conservatory with **Gabriel Fauré** until World War I when he joined the Navy. After the war, he re-entered the conservatory and was awarded the *Prix de Rome* in 1919.
- During his three-year (1920–22) stay in Rome, he wrote two works that made him famous: *Escales* (Ports of Call) for orchestra and *Histoires* (Stories) for piano solo. *Histoires* is a set of 10 short pieces with descriptive titles. Best known of the set is *Le petit âne blanc* (The Little White Donkey), which the composer later arranged for piano duet and others transcribed for solo violin, cello, flute, bassoon and saxophone.

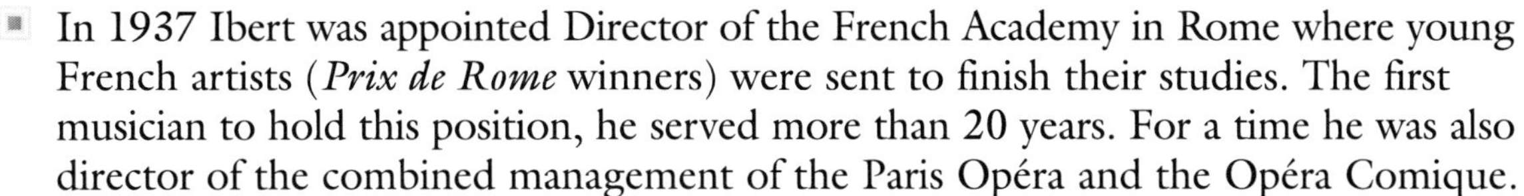

- In 1937 Ibert was appointed Director of the French Academy in Rome where young French artists (*Prix de Rome* winners) were sent to finish their studies. The first musician to hold this position, he served more than 20 years. For a time he was also director of the combined management of the Paris Opéra and the Opéra Comique.

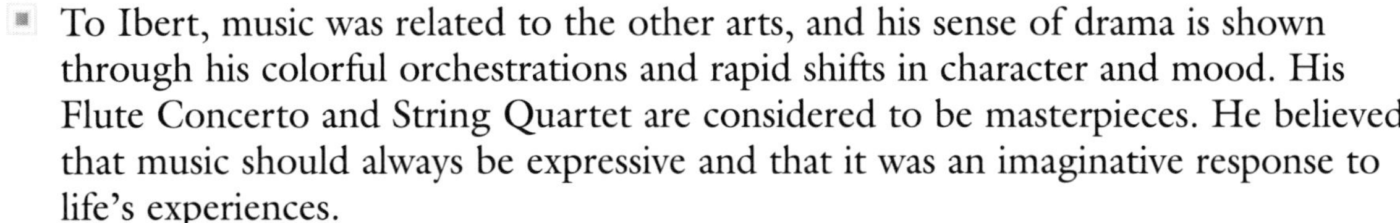

- To Ibert, music was related to the other arts, and his sense of drama is shown through his colorful orchestrations and rapid shifts in character and mood. His Flute Concerto and String Quartet are considered to be masterpieces. He believed that music should always be expressive and that it was an imaginative response to life's experiences.

[23] *New Grove Dictionary*, s.v. "Jacques Ibert."

A Giddy Girl is the fourth in the *Histoires* set and the only one that does not have a French title. A clue to Ibert's reasoning could be in the opening instructions to the performer, *"in the style of a sentimental English romance."* Like Debussy's *Préludes*, the titles in this set are at the end of each piece. Some definitions for the word "giddy" are a lighthearted or dizzy sensation, frivolous, unstable or foolish. The many tempo and dynamic changes in the score help depict this flighty female.

A Giddy Girl

Jacques Ibert (1890–1962)
Histoires, No. 4

15
m.g.
cédez et diminuez
(slower and softer)
en exagérant les nuances
(exaggerate the nuances)
18
au mouv^t
pp
poco
21
un peu retenu
au mouv^t
24
cresc.
m.g.
f
27

"I know ... I have [not] made harmonic innovations, ...but I think there's room for ***new*** *music, which doesn't mind using other people's chords. Wasn't that the case with Mozart—Schubert?"*

Francis Poulenc[24]

Francis Poulenc (1899–1963)

At first seen as just a fashionable composer whose music reflected the spirit of Paris in the 1920s, **Francis Poulenc** developed an individual style that connected with audiences, and he became a leader in contemporary French music.

- Born into a wealthy family of manufacturers, serious music study was not encouraged, so Poulenc's mother gave him his early training. After World War I, he became associated with *Les Six*, a group of musicians that included **Georges Auric** (1899–1983), **Louis Durey** (1888–1979), **Arthur Honegger** (1892–1955), **Darius Milhaud** (1892–1974), Poulenc, and **Germaine Tailleferre** (1892–1983), who were rejecting both Romantic and Impressionistic styles and preferred the simplicity and humor of **Eric Satie**. They were the "moderns" of the 1920s who were blending "serious" music with jazz, music hall, vaudeville, and commercial music.
- Largely self-taught as a composer, Poulenc began formal composition lessons in 1921 when he already had successful publications. His gift for writing unpretentious, yet beautiful melodies was recognized by **Maurice Ravel**, who envied Poulenc's ability to *"write his own folk songs."*[25] His about 130 art songs are cited among the greatest of the century.
- Poulenc's Roman Catholic faith was restored in 1935 after a close friend was killed in an automobile accident. As a result, he began composing music based on sacred themes, creating his popular *Gloria* for choir and orchestra. His opera about nuns martyred during the French Revolution, *Les Dialogues des Carmélites,* is one of the few contemporary operas in the international repertoire.
- Poulenc's works for piano include about 90 solo pieces, a concerto, and a two-piano concerto, with his personal favorites being the 15 *Improvisations.* Although not his deepest music, the piano pieces give pleasure to both the listener and performer.

Les groupe des six *by Jacques-Emile Blanche (1861–1942)*

Germaine Tailleferre, seated left; Darius Milhaud, seated left, facing front; Arthur Honegger, seated left, facing right; Francis Poulenc, standing right, head inclined; Georges Auric, seated right. Louis Durey is absent. Singer Jane Bathori (1877–1970), in the center, premiered many of their works. Jean Cocteau (1889–1963), who collaborated with them, is on the far right.

In 1918, Poulenc's witty set of three *Mouvements perpétuels* (Perpetual Movements) became a hit with amateur pianists throughout Europe. The unusual ending of this piece is typical of Poulenc's writing style and has been described as "urban irony."

[24] *New Grove Dictionary,* s.v. "Francis Poulenc."

[25] <http://www.chesternovello.com/composer/1265/main.html>

Mouvements perpétuels No. 2

Francis Poulenc
(1899–1963)

ⓐ The editor suggests all grace notes be played before the beat.

"Pay no attention to what the critics say; there has never been a statue set up in honor of a critic."
Jean Sibelius, Finnish composer[26]

Scandinavian and Finnish Music

During the 19th century, the trend for collecting native folk material influenced Scandinavian musicians, but they still traveled to Germany for serious study. Norwegian **Edvard Grieg** (1843–1907) and Finnish **Jean Sibelius** (1865–1957) gained international fame with compositions that synthesized their German training with national music. Because of the intense nationalistic reaction, public performances of Sibelius's *Finlandia* (1899) were banned by the Russian government that ruled Finland until it became independent in 1917.

Selim Palmgren (1878–1951)

Courtesy of the Sibley Music Library, Eastman School of Music, University of Rochester

Sometimes referred to as "The Finnish Chopin," **Selim Palmgren** was a virtuoso pianist, choral and instrumental conductor, and composition teacher. He wrote over 700 works, including 300 piano miniatures and five piano concertos. His piano style is late Romantic infused with folk themes and Impressionistic techniques.

- Born in the lumber region of southern Finland, his sister, who had studied piano at the Leipzig Conservatory, was his first teacher. When he enrolled in the Helsinki Conservatory, he absorbed the culture of the city and heard many touring artists who stopped there on their way to St. Petersburg, Russia.
- In the mid-19th century, epic folk poems, chants and songs from throughout Finland were published in a collection known as *Kalevala*. Palmgren used these elements in his compositions, including *Daniel Hjort* (1910), an opera based on historical events in 16th-century Finland. It was well received and established him as an important composer.
- He toured Europe and the United States as a pianist, and in 1923 he was invited to teach at the Eastman School of Music in Rochester, New York. He taught there until 1927 and in Helsinki from 1936–51 at what is known today as the Sibelius Academy.

[26] Watson, *Dictionary of Musical Quotations,* 382.

Palmgren's love of nature is reflected in the pictorial titles of many of his piano works: *The River, The Sea, The Isle of Shadows, Dragonfly, Bird-Song,* and his best-known piece, *May Night*. Palmgren's use of the Impressionistic techniques of **ostinato** (repeated) **chords**, the **whole-tone scale**, and **unresolved chords moving in parallel motion** help create the mysterious atmosphere and beauty of an evening in May.

May Night

Selim Palmgren (1878–1951)
Op. 27, No. 4

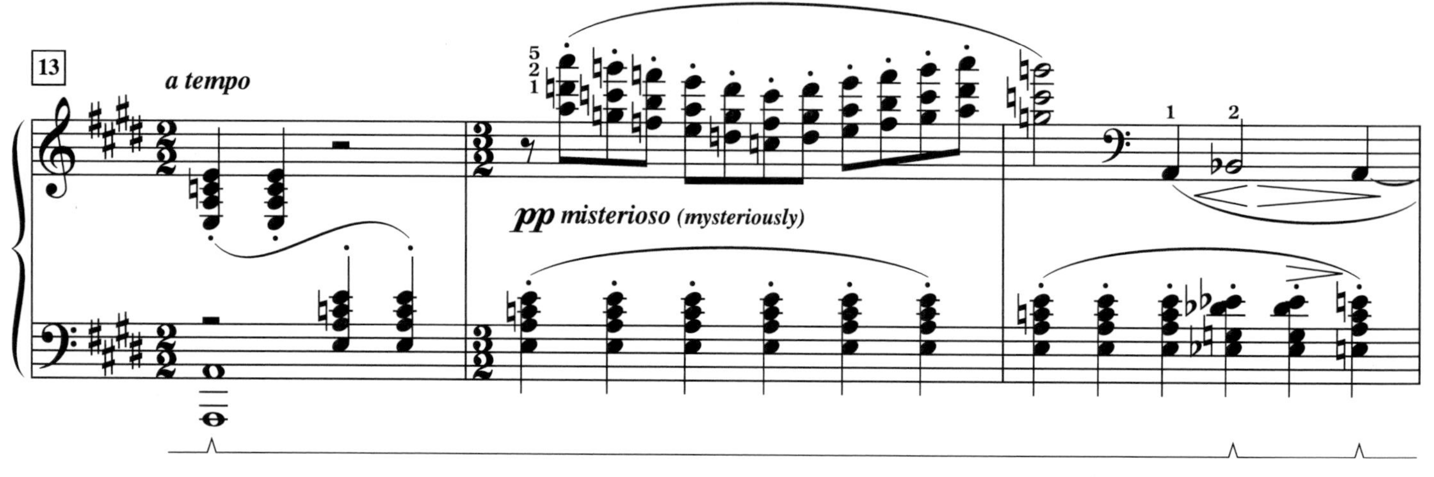
13
a tempo
pp misterioso (mysteriously)

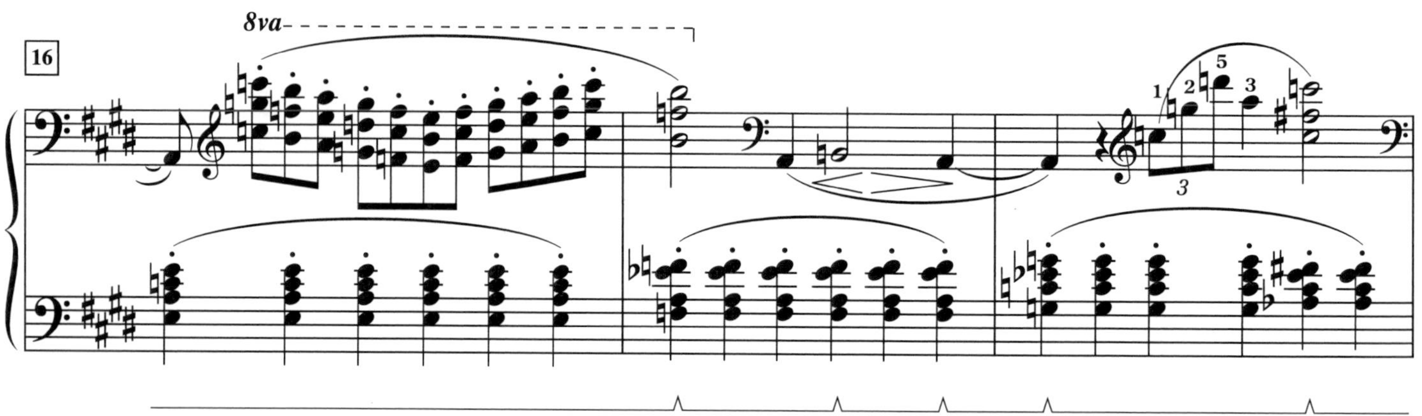
16
8va

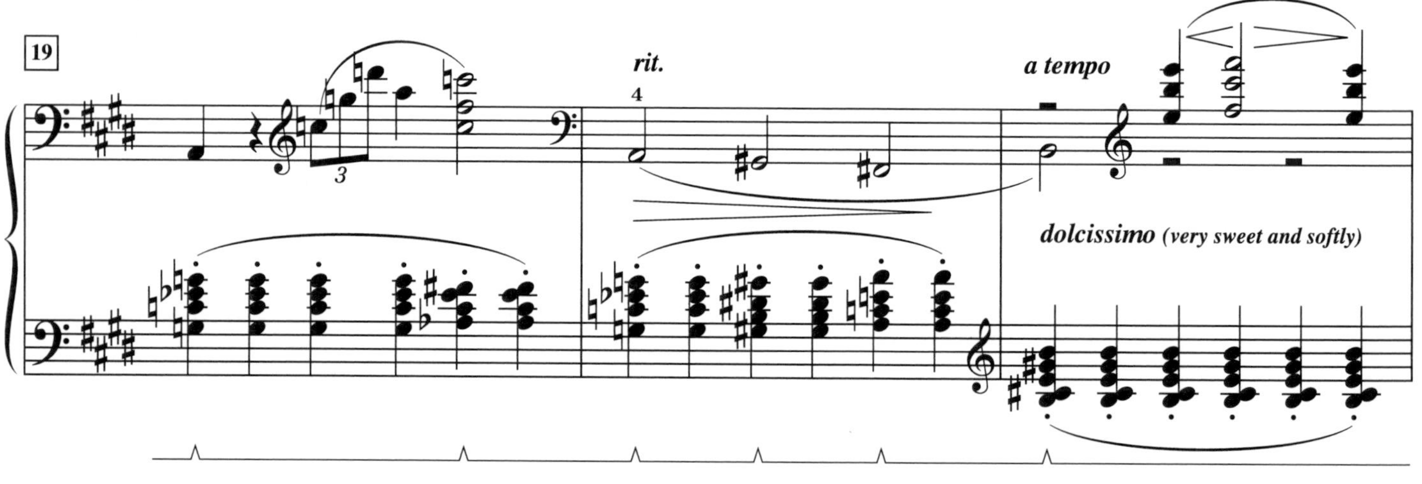
19
rit.
a tempo
dolcissimo (very sweet and softly)

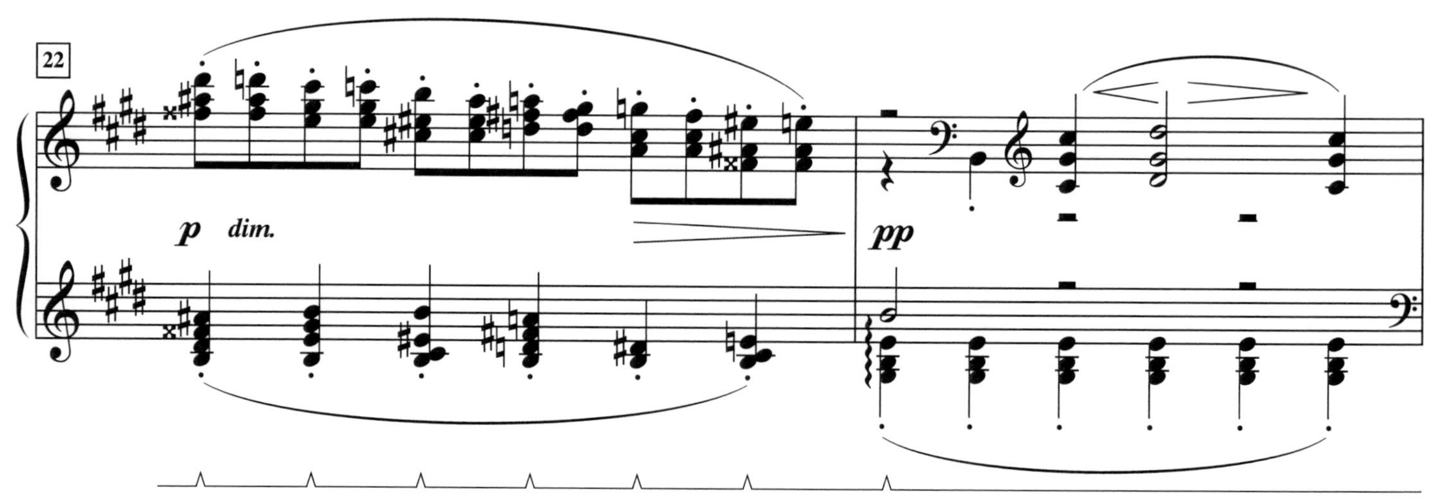
22
p dim.
pp

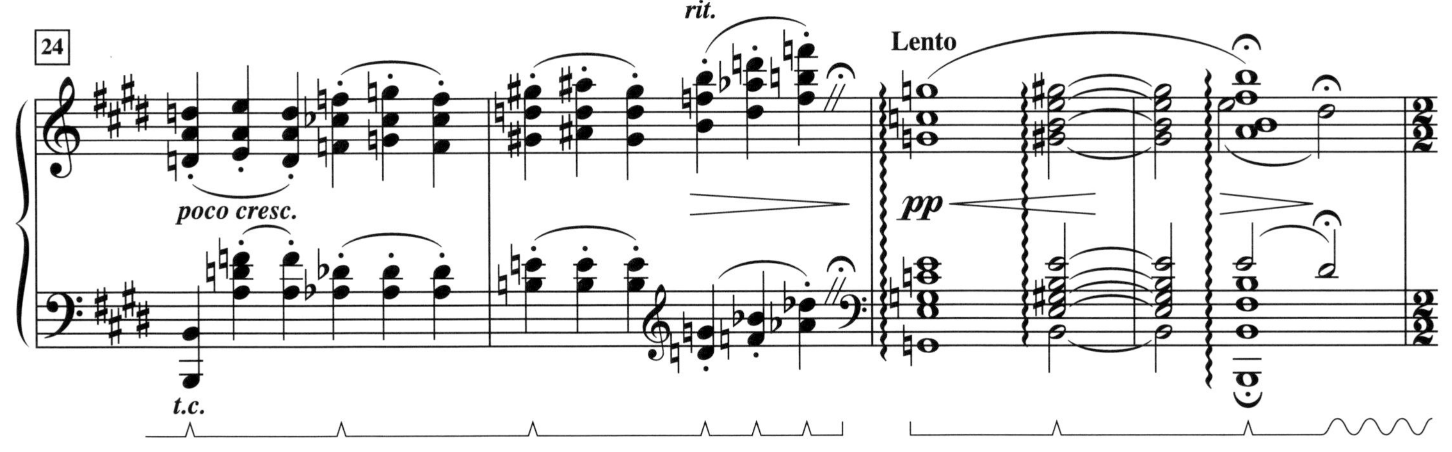
24
rit.
Lento
poco cresc.
pp
t.c.

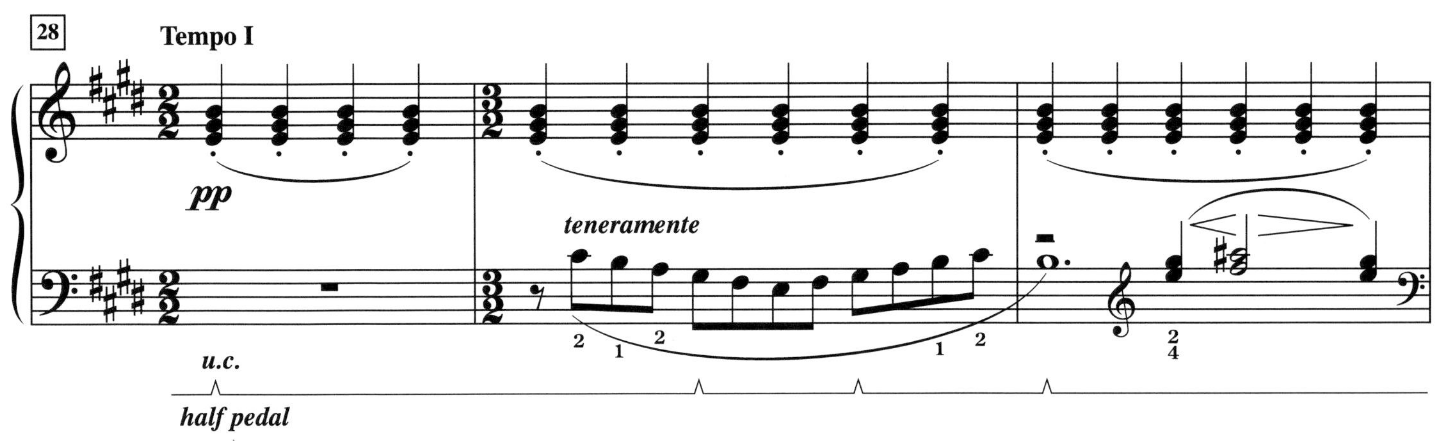
28
Tempo I
pp
teneramente
u.c.
half pedal

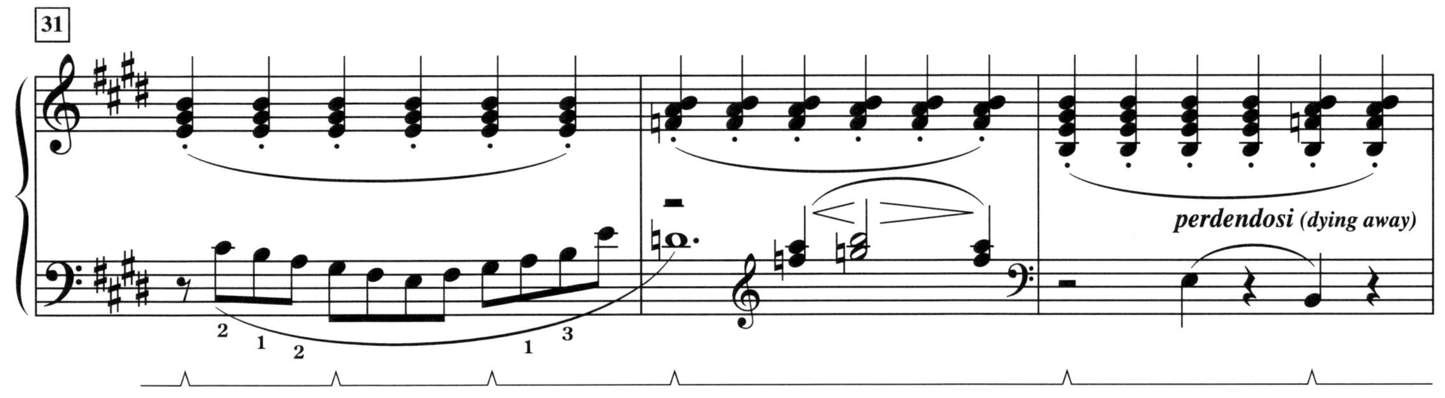
31
perdendosi (dying away)

34
poco rall.
ppp

"Hungary is my homeland ... I .am part of the national pride."
Franz Liszt (1811–1886), pianist and composer[27]

Hungarian Music

Ede Poldini

The Hapsburg family in Vienna, Austria, ruled Hungary from 1686 until the early 20th century, giving Hungarian art music a strong Austro-German influence. **Franz Joseph Haydn** (1732–1809) spent most of his life on the Hungarian estates of his employer, the German-speaking Esterházy family. In the tide of 19th-century nationalism, there was a demand for opera in the Hungarian language, some folk materials were compiled, and conservatories were founded so students would not have to go abroad for study.

Ede (Eduard) Poldini (1869–1957)

Ede Poldini was known in his native Hungary primarily for his operas and operettas, although he also wrote many works for choir, solo voice, and piano. In the rest of the world, he was most famous for his numerous short piano pieces. His *Poupée valsante* (Dancing Doll) was an international hit in family parlors in the early 20th century. *Scare Crow* (page 48) is typical of his more than 100 colorful and effective works for piano solo.

- Born in Budapest, Poldini studied at the National Conservatory as well as in Vienna and then spent a year in Geneva, Switzerland. He moved permanently to Switzerland in 1908, but he still received awards from the Hungarian government, including the Hungarian Medal for Artists in 1948.

Budapest Opera House

- Poldini wrote at least seven operas, and *Wedding in Carnival Time* was his most popular. Written in Hungarian, it has been described as a combination of German and French comic opera styles blended with Hungarian elements. One critic wrote that the folk themes were simply decoration while it was highly praised by others. It was performed in about 20 European cities including London where it was titled *Love Adrift*.

[27] Alan Walker, *Franz Liszt, the Virtuoso Years* (Ithaca, NY: Cornell University Press, 1983), 48.

"As I went from village to village, I heard the true music of my race… This music was a revelation to me."
Béla Bartók[28]

Béla Bartók (1881–1945)

Béla Bartók was recognized as a virtuoso pianist who had gained international respect for his scholarly research on native folk music. The general public, however, did not accept his compositions until after his death, and he died in a state of near poverty—an ironic ending in the Romantic tradition to one of the most progressive 20th-century composers.

- While a student at the Budapest Academy of Music, it was expected he would have a career as a virtuoso pianist. He specialized in the music of fellow Hungarian Franz Liszt and joined the academy piano faculty soon after graduating.
- In 1905 he experienced a "second birth" when he discovered the music of peasants. For nine years he traveled extensively, recording folk tunes that he then transcribed and published. This music so permeated Bartók that his compositions were filled with "imaginary folk tunes"—original music with irregular, stabbing rhythms, haunting melodies, and dissonant harmonies.
- His piano music explored the percussive rather than the lyrical aspects of the instrument. *Allegro barbaro* (1911) was described as having "savage energy and primitivism," and Bartók, *"if not stark mad, certainly [was] an eccentric person."*[29] Many consider his *Mikrokosmos* (Little World), to be his most significant work for piano. Originally written for his son Péter (b. 1924), it contains 153 progressive piano pieces in six volumes that teach technique, national styles, and 20th-century compositional devices.
- In 1940 he settled in New York City where his last years were filled with homesickness, artistic frustration and illness. Although respected by most professionals, his music was seldom performed. Fatally ill with leukemia, the final measures of his third (and most popular) piano concerto were finished from sketches. A few months after his death, his works were being frequently performed throughout the world, and still are.

Photo: Tamas Fener
By permission from the Kodaly Institute, Kecskemet, Hungary

Béla Bartók (second from left) and his assistant Ahmed Adnan Saygun (1907–1991), with an Edison recorder in a 1936 folk-song collecting trip in Anatolia, Turkey

[28] *Colour Library Book of Great Composers* (London: Marshall Cavendish Ltd., 1989), 407.

[29] Philip Hale quoted in *Milton Cross New Encyclopedia of the Great Composers and Their Music, vol. 1* (Garden City, New York: Doubleday & Company, Inc., 1969), 59.

Some Articulation Markings in Bartók[30]

▾	*Staccatissimo*	As short as possible with a percussive touch.
•	*Staccato*	About half the written value of the note.
–	*Tenuto*	Almost full value; key is pressed, not struck.
⸗	*Dotted tenuto*	Never less than half value; key is pressed.

Dynamic Accents in Diminishing Emphasis

Bartók playing on a Hungarian hurdy-gurdy in 1908 in his Budapest home surrounded by peasant furniture from Transylvania

Joc cu Bâtă (Stick Dance) is the first of six *Rumanian Folk Dances.* Originally written for piano, Bartók also transcribed them for violin and for orchestra.

Joc cu Bâtă

Béla Bartók (1881–1945)
Sz. 56, No. 1

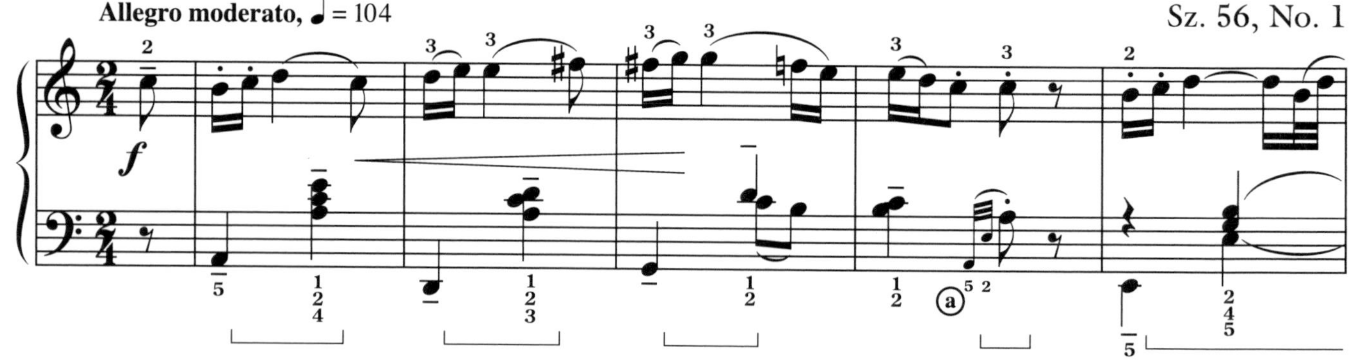

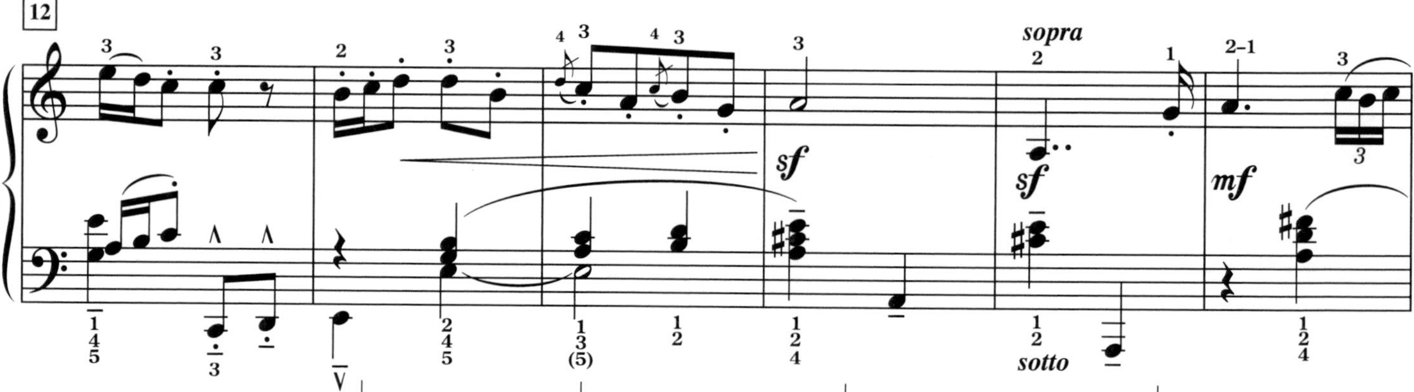

ⓐ The editor suggests all grace notes be played before the beat.

[30] Benjamin Suchoff, *Guide to Bartók's Mikrokosmos* (New York: Boosey & Hawkes, 1971), 14–15.

18
cresc. molto
24
30
sopra
sotto
36
42
sf poco allarg.

Scare Crow

Ede (Eduard) Poldini (1869–1957)
Op. 30, No. 3

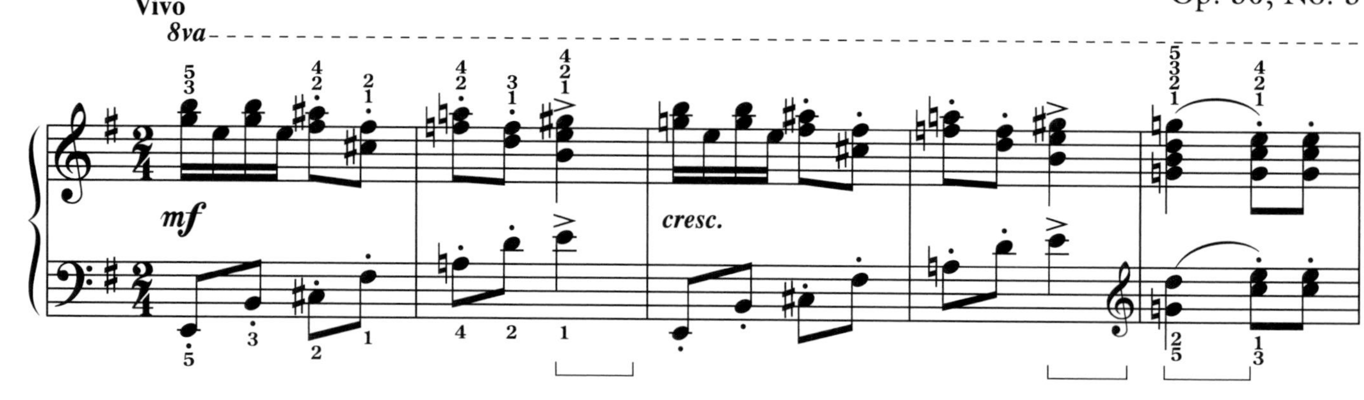

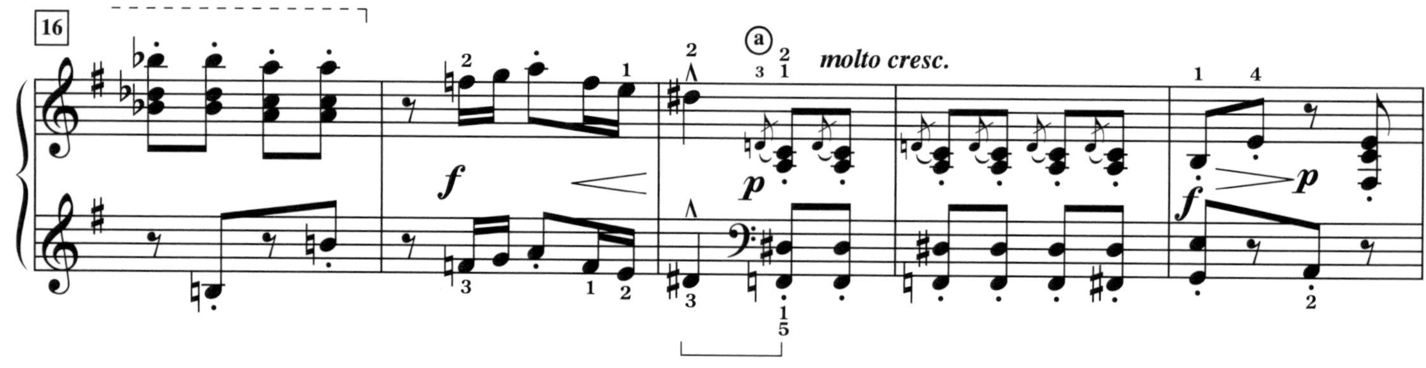

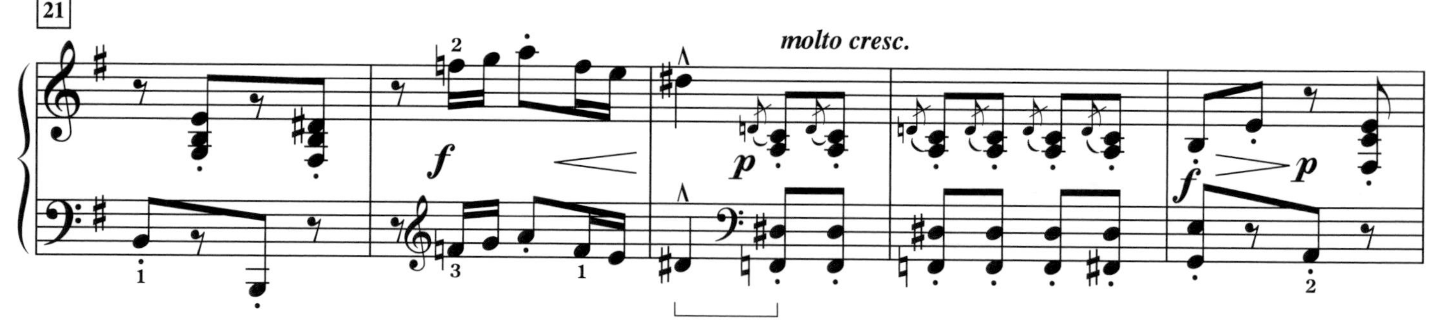

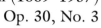

ⓐ The editor suggests all grace notes be played before the beat.

26
31
8va
to Coda
8va
cresc.
sf
p
rall.
p
RH 1
37
a tempo
42
a tempo
rit.
mf
cresc.
47
ff
p rall.

53
a tempo
59
rit.
a tempo
mf
cresc.
64
D.C. al Coda
ff
Coda
8va
cresc.
73
ff accel.
sff

[Nazareth] "The true incarnation of the Brazilian musical soul."
Heitor Villa-Lobos (1887–1959), Brazilian composer[31]

Americas' Music

Music in South and Central America shows a strong European influence, especially from France and Spain, probably due to years of colonization. Other influences in the region were Negro and native Indian elements. Blending music from the three continents of Europe, South America and Africa created unique rhythms, popular dances, ragtime, and jazz styles.

Ernesto Nazareth (1863–1934)

Ernesto Nazareth was the most famous popular Brazilian pianist of the 20th century. Most of his around 200 piano compositions were short dances: waltzes, polkas, quadrilles and tangos. He created a unique piano style with his native Brazilian folk materials, and some of his pieces became popular in Europe. In this way he was like **Scott Joplin** (1868–1917) in the United States, who was writing his internationally known piano rags about the same time.

- Born in Rio de Janeiro, Nazareth's mother gave him his first piano lessons and also encouraged him to improvise. When he was only 14, a polka he composed was published. In 1903, he needed money so badly he sold a piece, *Brejeiro,* for a small sum. Although it became popular internationally, he never received additional fees.

The Odeon Cinema in Rio de Janeiro

- Nazareth earned his living at various times by teaching, playing for private parties, and by playing piano sheet music in a department store. People would come in and select music to purchase after listening to him play. He was an excellent sight-reader.
- He also performed at the best movie theater in town, the Odeon. Moviegoers would arrive an hour before the movie began to listen to performances by him and a small orchestra. He played music of European masters as well as his own compositions.
- Personal health problems and the death of his wife and daughter contributed to his having a mental breakdown, and he was sent to an institution. Missing one day, he was found drowned in a nearby lake.

31 <http://www.bn.br/extra/musica/enaz_lis.htm>

Nazareth gave most of his pieces both a **title** and a **subtitle**. Titles usually stated a mood and were sometimes humorous, such as *Things Could Be Worse*; or commentary such as *Naughty* or *The Most Elegant One*. His most common subtitle is "tango." In Brazil when asked, "How are things going?" a common response is *Remando* (translated "Getting By"). That is the title of this tango. According to reports of Nazareth's playing, the score was not precisely notated, and he used *rubato* to create a smooth, sophisticated, "delicious" style.

Remando Tango

Ernesto Nazareth
(1863–1934)

19
24
29
cresc.
f
dim.
34
1.
2.
mf
p
39
1.

44
2.
48
mf
52
f
56
61
1.
2.
D.S. al Fine
p

"He [Villa-Lobos] was, in short, Brazil in music."
David Ewen (1907–1985), music historian[32]

Heitor Villa-Lobos (1887–1959)

Heitor Villa-Lobos was the first South American composer to gain international fame, honors and awards. Largely self-taught, he fused European classical music with a variety of Brazilian elements in his about 2,000 works that include over 200 pieces for piano.

- Villa-Lobos's father died when he was 12. After that, he earned his own living by playing piano, guitar and cello in restaurants, theaters and movie houses. He enrolled briefly at the National Music Institute but preferred to study treatises and scores of great masters on his own.
- The first of many trips to jungles and other parts of Brazil was in 1912 to study Indian music, rites, myths, folk songs and dances. Colorful stories of his experiences included capture by cannibals who released him only after he played the cello! When questioned about finding music that had "virtually disappeared," he replied, *"Parrots heard ancient melodies and sang them to me."*[33]
- When pianist **Artur Rubinstein** (1887–1982) began programming *A prole do bebê* (figuratively translated as "The Baby's Toys"), Villa-Lobos's fame spread abroad. He traveled to Paris in 1923, and his exotic music created a sensation and generated invitations for appearances throughout Europe.
- In 1930 as Director of Music Education for Rio de Janeiro, he revolutionized the teaching of music, making it required in schools with emphasis on folk song and choral singing. He founded the Brazilian Academy of Music in 1950, was its president, and conducted his works internationally until his death.
- Villa-Lobos's most famous work for piano is the seventh piece from *A prole do bebê no. 1*,[34] a set of eight pieces, each representing a type of doll. *O polichinelo* depicts the popular clown-puppet, Punch, a likable rogue who carried a stick and had a habit of knocking over anyone who disagreed with him. The **polytonality** of left-hand black-key pentatonic figures against right-hand diatonic C-major figures gives high energy and excitement.

Punch, the clown

[32] David Ewen, *The World of Twentieth Century Music* (Englewood Cliffs, NJ: Prentice-Hall, Inc., 1970), 872.

[33] David and Martha Appleby, "The Legend of Villa-Lobos," *Clavier Magazine* (March 1987): 20.

[34] Villa-Lobos wrote three sets of piano pieces entitled *A prole do bebê*.

O polichinelo

Heitor Villa-Lobos (1887–1959)
A prole do bebê no. 1

Vivo

col pedal sempre ⓐ

ⓐ Villa-Lobos indicated ***col pedal sempre*** (with pedal always). The editor suggests to use shallow pedal throughout the piece to add color to the tone without excessive blurring.

19
sf
23
28
le chant bien distinct
(bring out the melody)
p
33
38

ⓑ This curved line indicates that the note should continue to sound. Keeping the damper pedal depressed will allow the strings to vibrate and continue to ring.

[After he performed at the White House] "It's only about 50 miles from the house where I was born, but it's a million miles in class."

Eubie Blake[35]

James Hubert "Eubie" Blake (1883–1983)

The son of former slaves, **Eubie Blake** paved the way for the equal acceptance of blacks in American entertainment. He wrote over 300 songs and instrumental pieces, music for six musical comedies and performed as a jazz pianist throughout his long life.

- When Blake began picking out tunes on a department store organ at age three, his mother agreed to pay twenty-five cents a week until the seventy-five dollar cost of the instrument was paid. He played music that he heard, and a local musician taught him theory and musical notation. When his mother told him to "Take that ragtime out of my house," he finally knew the name of the style he was playing.

Eubie Blake at the piano with Noble Sissle

- As a teenager, he performed in saloons on piano, as a melodeon player for a traveling medicine show, and as a dancer in a black minstrel show in New York City. In his twenties, he accompanied singers, played his own solos in Atlantic City, and began collaborating with the singer-lyricist **Noble Sissle** (1889–1975). They wrote hit songs, and as the "Dixie Duo" were one of the first successful African-American acts to play the white vaudeville circuit and to perform in Europe.
- In 1921 they wrote and starred in *Shuffle Along*, the first hit Broadway production written, directed, performed, and produced by black Americans. It introduced jazz dancing and grossed over eight million dollars. A song from the show, *I'm Just Wild about Harry*, was revived during the 1948 presidential campaign of **Harry Truman** (1884–1972). Eubie enrolled at New York University and completed a degree in composition in 1950.
- With renewed interest in ragtime, he performed at a Ragfest in St. Louis at the age of 83. It was reported that he outplayed all the younger pianists, sparking his second career as a performer, lecturer and personality. He played in Carnegie Hall and Town Hall, on PBS specials, at festivals throughout the United States and Europe, with the Boston Pops orchestra, and appeared 40 times on the Tonight Show with **Johnny Carson** (b. 1925).
- After receiving eight honorary doctorates, he was asked at age 96 how he felt about his new academic credentials. *"I guess now I won't have any trouble getting a job."*[36]

[35] Al Rose, *Eubie Blake* (New York: Schirmer Books, 1979), 164.

[36] Ibid., 51.

Blake's wife was a classically trained pianist. A few years after their marriage, Joseph W. Stern & Co. published *The Chevy Chase* fox-trot and *Fizz Water* rag (1914). Blake sold these pieces to the publisher without "mechanical rights" (rights for phonographs and piano rolls), a mistake which prevented him from receiving thousands of dollars in royalties. *The Chevy Chase* has dramatic pauses in the rhythmic flow.

The Chevy Chase Fox-Trot

James Hubert "Eubie" Blake
(1883–1983)

22
f
p
26
f
p
30
f
34
rit.
38
a tempo
p

42
f
p
46
f
50
54
mf
58
8va

62
66
70
TRIO
74
78

82
86
91
95
99
103
1.
2.
f